and the Market
1815–1848

Sean Wilentz

Historical Association

SEAN WILENTZ, Professor of History at Princeton University, is the author of *Chants Democratic: New York City & the Rise of the American Working Class, 1788–1850* (Oxford University Press, 1984). *Chants* has won several honors, including the American Historical Association's Albert Beveridge Award and the Organization of American Historians' Frederick Jackson Turner Award.

This essay originally appeared in *The New American History*, published by Temple University Press in the series Critical Perspectives on the Past, edited by Susan Porter Benson, Stephen Brier, and Roy Rosenzweig. Copyright © 1990 Temple University.

This edition published by the American Historical Association
ISBN: 0-87229-053-0
Printed in the United States of America

▶ Contents

▶ **Essays in** *The New American History* **series**

▶ Introduction

IN THE COURSE OF THE PAST TWENTY YEARS, AMERICAN HISTORY HAS BEEN remade. Inspired initially by the social movements of the 1960s and 1970s—which shattered the "consensus" vision that had dominated historical writing—and influenced by new methods borrowed from other disciplines, American historians redefined the very nature of historical study. The rise of the "new histories," the emphasis on the experience of ordinary Americans, the impact of quantification and cultural analysis, the eclipse of conventional political and intellectual history—these trends are now so widely known (and the subject of such controversy) that they need little reiteration. The study of American history today looks far different than it did a generation ago.

This series comprises essays written by thirteen scholars—many of whom have been at the forefront of the transformation of historical study—each assessing recent developments in historians' understanding of a period or a major theme in the nation's past. The idea for the collection originated with a request from the American Historical Association for a series of pamphlets addressed specifically to high school teachers of American history and designed to familiarize them with the most up-to-date historical scholarship.

After a false start or two the proposal, somewhat revised, was adopted and published as a collection by Temple University Press, and now, separately, by the AHA. *The New American History* is addressed to a wide audience: students, teachers, and the broad public concerned with the current state of American historical study.

Each author was given a free hand in developing his or her reflections. No attempt has been made to fit the essays into a predetermined mold or impose a single point of view or interpretive framework. Nonetheless, certain themes recur with remarkable regularity, demonstrating how pervasively the "new histories" have reshaped our understanding of the American past.

If anything is characteristic of the recent study of American history, it is attention to the experience of previously neglected groups—not simply as an addition to a preexisting body of knowledge but as a fundamental redefinition of history itself. Women's history has greatly expanded its subject area, moving beyond the movement for suffrage, which preoccupied earlier women historians, into such previously ignored realms as the history of sexuality. Labor history, from a field that defined its subject as the experience of wage workers in factories and the activities of unionized workers, has expanded to encompass the study of slaves, women at home, and the majority of laborers, who in America have always been unorganized.

Even more striking, perhaps, is that African-American history and women's history have matured to the point where they are not widely recognized as legitimate subfields with their own paradigms and debates but are seen as indispensable to any understanding of the broad American experience. These points are made effectively in surveys of the two fields by Thomas Holt and Linda Gordon, but they are evident in other contributions as well. Richard McCormick makes clear that any calculus of Americans' gains and losses in the late nineteenth and early twentieth centuries must take into account the severe reverses suffered by blacks in those years. William Chafe places the civil rights movement at the center of his analysis of social change in post–World War II America. My own essay on the Civil War era argues not only that slavery and emancipation were the central issues in the sectional crisis but that blacks were active agents in shaping the era's history.

Women's history, too, has forced historians not simply to compensate for their previous neglect of one-half of the population but to rethink some of their basic premises. Linda Kerber delineates how the

American Revolution affected prevailing definitions of "manhood" and "womanhood" and how patriarchy itself was restructured as a result of the revolutionary crisis. Leon Fink emphasizes the obvious but long-ignored fact that women have always been part of the country's labor history. Sean Wilentz shows that a key result of economic changes in the Jacksonian era was an ideological division between the public sphere of men and the private sphere of women.

Many of the essays also demonstrate the impact of new methods on recent historical study. John Murrin shows how historical demography has yielded a new estimate of the human toll exacted by the colonization of the New World and how epidemiology affects our understanding of the decimation of the hemisphere's original inhabitants. Alice Kessler-Harris outlines the ways in which the "new empiricism" of statistical analysis has helped shape developments in social history. Richard McCormick and Alan Brinkley assess the impact of modernization theory on the study of both pre– and post–World War I periods.

Despite the apparent ascendancy of social history, these essays do not lend credence to recent complaints that historians are no longer concerned with politics, economics, the Constitution, and intellectual history. Such traditional concerns appear in virtually every essay, although often in forms that earlier historians might find unrecognizable. The old "presidential synthesis"—which understood the evolution of American society chiefly via presidential elections and administrations—is dead (and not lamented). And "politics" now means much more than the activities of party leaders. Some essays devote attention to the broad political culture or "public life" of a particular era; others stress the role of the state itself in American history and the ways various groups have tried to use it for their own purposes.

Alan Brinkley, for example, discusses the New Deal within the context of the constraints imposed on government by the nature of America's political and economic institutions, and the general impact of the period on the evolution of the American state. And Walter LaFeber shows how the Constitution has helped to shape the evolution of American foreign policy.

Many historians have lamented of late the failure of the current generation of scholars to produce a modern "synthesis" of the American past. Older synthetic interpretations, ranging from Frederick Jackson Turner's frontier thesis to the consensus view of the 1950s, have been

x
ERIC FONER

shattered, but no new one has emerged to fill the void. Indeed, the very diversity of the "new histories" and the portrait of America they have created seem to have fragmented historical scholarship and impeded the attempt to create a coherent new vision of the national experience. Several of the essays echo this concern, but there is sufficient similarity in their approaches and interpretations to suggest that the fragmentation of historical study may have been overstated. If the essays do not, and by their very nature cannot, produce the widely called-for new synthesis, several do point in that direction. Sean Wilentz, for example, suggests that the social, political, and economic history of Jacksonian America can be integrated into a coherent whole by placing the market revolution at the center of the account. McCormick demonstrates that a "public life" can be a flexible, imaginative concept, capable of integrating a variety of social, economic, and political developments.

As this series demonstrates, American history is a field of remarkable diversity and vitality. Its practitioners continue to grapple with the most pressing issues and persistent themes of our national experience: definitions of liberty and equality, causes of social change, the exercise of political power. Today, popular knowledge—or lack of knowledge—of the nation's past has once again become a subject of intense public discussion. Certainly, the more all of us—students, teachers, and other citizens—know of our national experience, the better. But as these essays illustrate, American history at its best remains not simply a collection of facts, not a politically sanctioned listing of indisputable "truths," but an ongoing mode of collective self-discovery about the nature of our society.

ERIC FONER
Columbia University

▶ ▶ ▶ ▶ ▶ ▶ ▶ ▶ ▶ ▶ ▶ ▶ ▶ ▶ ▶

SOCIETY, POLITICS, AND THE MARKET REVOLUTION, 1815–1848

Sean Wilentz

FOR MANY YEARS, HISTORIANS HAD LITTLE DIFFICULTY FINDING LABELS TO DE-scribe the period from 1815 to 1848. To some it was the age of Jackson, dominated by Old Hickory and the Democratic party; to others, the era of the common man, a time of sweeping democratic ferment and reform. Today such phrases sound quaint. Two decades' worth of outstanding re-visionist work has made political historians wary of the old presidential synthesis of American history; less attention is now paid to the specific details of Jacksonian electioneering and policy-making, and more to such broad themes as the changing structure of party organizations and the rise of new political ideologies. Likewise, an outpouring of work by social historians—much of it on groups previously slighted—has dramatically changed basic assumptions about the period and raised new, often dis-turbing questions: How can the years that brought the rise of the Cotton Kingdom and the spread of slavery reasonably be called the era of the com-mon man? What was the role of women in this phase of American history? Were not at least some of the democratic advances of the time won at the murderous expense of Native Americans?

By exploring these and other issues, recent studies have moved well beyond the familiar chronicles of political and social elites. They have cast serious doubts on those "consensus" interpretations which assumed

1

that nineteenth-century Americans, whatever their differences, shared an attachment to liberal capitalist ideals. Unfortunately, recent work has fragmented our understanding into a host of academic subspecialties. It has also led, in some instances, to a denigration of formal politics and policy, as if such "traditional" matters as the Bank War or debates over the tariff were unimportant. The job of connecting the pieces—and especially of recombining social and political history—has only just begun. That job is made difficult by persisting scholarly disagreements over all sorts of interpretive issues. Still, one theme does seem to unite Jacksonian historians of various persuasions and suggest a way of once again viewing the period as a whole: the central importance of the market revolution, which, in one way or another, touched the lives of all Americans. As part of that revolution there arose new forms of social life, consciousness, and politics. These, in turn, prepared the way for the Civil War.

THE MARKET REVOLUTION

The extraordinary economic changes of the early nineteenth century have never failed to impress historians. Between 1815 and 1850 Americans constructed elaborate networks of roads, canals, and early railroad lines; opened up wide areas of newly acquired land for settlement and trade; and began to industrialize manufacturing. What had been in Thomas Jefferson's day a backward rural nation on the fringes of world economic development had by midcentury established many of the preconditions necessary to its becoming a major economic power.

In the 1950s George Rogers Taylor wrote what remains the authoritative account of these changes and dubbed them, collectively, America's "transportation revolution." Since then, historians have done less to challenge Taylor's interpretation than to reexamine some of its implications. Social historians in particular have stressed that economic change radically disrupted existing systems of production and old social hierarchies, replacing them with entirely new opportunities and dependencies. Behind the technological and institutional innovations Taylor discussed was a deeper revolution in human relations, linked to the emergence of new markets in land, labor, and produce.

Much of the scholarly work on this market revolution has concentrated on northeastern cities as key sites of economic development. Intense mercantile activity there, of course, long antedated 1815. Yet between 1815 and 1850 eastern urban capitalists dramatically accelerated the pace of economic change. Often working hand in hand with state and local governments, these merchant capitalists were at the forefront of transportation improvements; they made great strides in expanding credit and financing resources and in imposing some order on currency and banking; above all, they hastened the erosion of the old artisan handicraft system and the rise of new manufacturing enterprises.

Compared to later periods in U.S. history, industrial growth between 1815 and 1848 was modest; by 1850, the majority of the nation's population still lived in rural areas and worked in agriculture, while only about 14 percent of the labor force worked in manufacturing. Nevertheless, the rate of industrial growth was impressive, especially in the Northeast. The most spectacular examples of early industrialization were the new textile mills of New England, financed by leading established seaboard merchants. Yet as labor historians have shown, mechanization and factory construction constituted only one of several strategies used to revamp manufacturing. In once bucolic single-industry towns (for example, the shoemaking center, Lynn, Massachusetts) merchant capitalists altered production by dividing up craft skills and putting out as much work as possible to country girls living in outlying rural communities. Entrepreneurs in the major seaboard cities and in newer inland settlements such as Cincinnati likewise divided up artisan crafts and relied on underpaid outworkers—women, children, poor immigrants—to produce work for low piece rates. The deployment of these different methods of production brought a rapid increase in the output of raw materials and finished goods, at lower prices and of a higher quality than Americans had ever enjoyed. Simultaneously, however, the new order disrupted the customary artisan regime of masters, journeymen, and apprentices and left thousands of workers dependent on the caprices of the wage-labor market.

Changes in northeastern manufacturing were closely related to a deepening crisis in northeastern rural life. Traditionally, historians slighted the extent of social change in the American countryside before the Civil War. Although improvements in transportation and increased commercialization obviously enlarged the productive capacity of American agriculture, historians tended to assume that most family farms were small capitalist enterprises from at least the mid-eighteenth century on. Recent scholarship, however, has focused on the variety of social pressures, beginning in the 1750s and continuing through the 1840s, that undermined a distinct way of life, one geared more to barter exchange and quasi-self-sufficiency than to the production of cash crops for market. At first, the major impetus for change was demographic, as the mounting population of the settled rural Northeast began to outstrip the available supply of land, leaving rural patriarchs unable to pass on sufficient acreage to their sons. By 1815 these straitened circumstances had led to a steady decline in family size and to an increase in westward migration; it had also heightened farmers' need for cash to buy additional land, thus encouraging them to shift into cash-crop production. The transportation improvements of the next thirty years facilitated that shift and brought to the countryside (at steadily decreasing prices) manufactured articles previously unavailable in the hinterland. By 1850 the vast majority of northeastern farmers had reorganized their production toward cash crops and were depending on country merchants for household items and farm implements once produced at home.

Few historians would dispute that the market revolution brought substantial material benefits to most northeasterners, urban and rural. But the new abundance was hardly distributed equally. Studies of property holding have confirmed that in small country towns and in large cities alike, a tiny proportion of the northeastern population came to command the bulk of the newly created wealth. Those who benefited most from the market revolution—merchants and manufacturers, lawyers and other professionals, and successful commercial farmers, along with their families— faced life situations very different from those known to earlier generations. The decline of the household as the locus of production led directly to a growing impersonality in the economic realm; household heads, instead of directing family enterprises or small shops, often had to find ways to recruit and discipline a wage-labor force; in all cases, they had to stay abreast of or even surpass their competitors.

Perhaps the most profound set of social changes confronting this new middle class involved the internal dynamics of family life. As Nancy Cott, Mary Ryan, and others have explained, the commercialization of both city and countryside removed women from the production of goods, including goods for strictly household use. The world of the propertied began to separate into two spheres: a male public sphere of politics, business, and the market, and a female private sphere of domestic duties and child rearing. By 1850 a new romantic standard of rights and responsibilities within middle-class families had replaced the more severe patriarchal regime of the eighteenth century—a "cult of domesticity" that vaunted women's supposed moral superiority while it restricted women's place to the home, as wives, mothers, and domestic guardians.

Less fortunate northeasterners faced a very different reality, dominated by the new dependencies created by the market revolution. For those at the bottom—immigrant and black day laborers, outwork seamstresses, the casual poor—a combination of overstocked labor markets and intense competition among employers kept wages and earnings near or below subsistence levels. Even in New England, farm girls who went off to work in factories expecting decent situations and high wages found that mill conditions had deteriorated by the mid-1830s. Those small independent artisans and well-paid craft workers who survived faced the real possibility of falling into similar distress, victimized as they were by an increasingly volatile business cycle and by the downward pressures on earnings and real wages in various important trades. By the 1830s a new working class was beginning to carve out its own identity in a variety of trade unions and in political efforts aimed at redirecting the course and consequences of American economic expansion. Marginal small farmers, their old networks of barter exchange undone, saw their livelihoods threatened by competition from western areas opened by canal development and by the middlemen's downward pressure on prices. To all these people, middle-class respectability and the cult of domesticity meant little when measured against the struggle to achieve or preserve their economic independence—or barring that, simply to make ends meet.

Far less is known about the market revolution's social impact in the Old Northwest and the western territories, although some fine recent work has started to redirect the field. Studies of migration suggest that rural northeasterners who could not make a go of it tried to avoid entering the urban wage-labor market; the largest single supply of urban workers (at least by 1850) consisted of immigrants and their children, among them hundreds of thousands of new arrivals escaping hard times in Ireland and Germany. Native-born rural northeasterners, joined by migrants from the South, headed west instead, most of them hoping to reconstruct the independent yeoman communities that had crumbled back home. Accordingly, they bought up as much cheap western land as they could to ensure that they would be able to provide for their families and their descendants.

This new yeomanry faced numerous obstacles. First, the removal of Native Americans from the land had to be completed; federal and state authorities willingly complied, using fraud and violence as necessary. Once the lands were open, settlers found themselves pitted against speculators eager to convert the virgin land to capitalist development. As the proportion of public land sold to speculators dramatically increased, would-be settlers and squatters had to battle hard to get the land they wanted. Once settled, farmers usually had to enter into some sort of economic relations with land speculators or bankers, either taking out mortgages or borrowing money to pay for farm improvements.

Despite these hardships, the vast majority of settlers eventually owned their farms outright. Most of them managed, for a time, to set up a facsimile of the yeoman regime. But it was not to last. Hoping to develop markets for their surplus crops, the western yeomen for the most part supported the extension of new east-west transport routes after 1820; the impact of their innovations quickly surpassed early expectations. By 1850 northwestern farm operators were almost fully integrated into commercial markets; specialized production of grain, livestock, or dairy products became the norm for successful commercial farmers. Under the pressure of reorganization, attempts to recreate the old order of yeoman independence collapsed. Although still dominated by small farmers, the Old Northwest emerged as one of the leading areas of cash-crop agriculture in the world, displacing New England and the mid-Atlantic seaboard as the supplier of eastern and overseas markets.

The opening of the market brought prosperity and rising profits to those farmers who secured sufficient acreage and learned to handle the new rules of credit and competition. Like eastern businessmen (and western businessmen in the new cities along the transport routes), western commercial farmers reordered their public and private lives in accord with the standards of eastern middle-class domesticity. Yet like the Northeast, the Northwest had its dispossessed and those who faced imminent dispossession. Not only were the Native Americans removed from their lands, but so too a substantial number of white settlers suffered from the revolution in marketing. Those unable to get sufficient credit to improve their operations or unwilling to learn capitalist agriculture methods wandered on the periphery of the most concentrated settlement, squatting on unimproved land or purchasing new land—often only to lose it. Those who could not sustain themselves and could not travel farther on fell into the ranks of agricultural wage labor. In all, the rise of capitalist agriculture in the Northwest, as in the Northeast, produced new classes of independent and dependent Americans.

The South experienced the market revolution quite differently, though just *how* differently has been the subject of continuing debate. The outstanding feature of southern economic and social history after 1815 was, of course, the rise of the Cotton Kingdom and the westward expansion of plantation slavery. Since the mid-1950s an outstanding literature on slavery has completely overturned the old sentimentalized, racist interpretation of the plantation as a benevolent institution, supposedly designed as much to civilize "inferior" blacks as to reap profits for the planters. Such recent historians as Eugene D. Genovese, Herbert G. Gutman, Lawrence Levine, and Albert Raboteau have paid especially close attention to the slaves' own experiences and discovered that a distinctive Afro-American culture took shape under slavery, a culture based on religious values and family ties that gave the slaves the power to endure and in certain ways resist the harshness of bondage. Far from a benign world of social harmony, the plantation South was an arena of intense day-to-day struggles between masters and slaves.

Far more controversial has been the argument, advanced most forcefully by Genovese, that the expansion of slavery led to the creation of a distinctive, noncapitalist southern civilization. As Genovese sees it, the southern slaveholders' attachment to land and slaves as their chief forms of investment guaranteed that the South would remain an economic backwater. To be sure, the slaveholders were linked to the wider world of capitalist markets and benefited from the improvement of American commerce and finance; like all men of business, they were acquisitive and at times greedy. But, Genovese contends, the master-slave relationship—so unlike labor relations in the North—created a unique mode of social organization and understanding. At the heart of these arrangements was what Genovese calls paternalism, a system of subordination that bound masters and slaves in an elaborate network of familial rights and duties. Plantation paternalism was fraught with conflict between master and slaves, although (Genovese insists) it did help contain the slaves' rebelliousness. Above all, the slaveholders as a class—and the South as a region—did not share in the possessive individualism and atomistic liberalism that were coming to dominate northern life.

Genovese's interpretation has been extremely influential, though it has also been challenged on various fronts. In particular, historians have questioned Genovese's contention that slavery precluded southern economic development, and that the planters exercised ideological hegemony over their slaves. Generally, however, scholars today agree that the market revolution had the effect of widening the differences between northern and southern society and culture. As historians examine the worlds of southerners who were neither masters nor slaves, southern distinctiveness seems all the more apparent; at the same time, these studies have heightened our appreciation of the complexities of the slave South.

Perhaps the most interesting work of the last few years concerns the nonslaveholders who constituted the majority of the southern white population before the Civil War. Far removed from the old settlements of the Tidewater and the rich soils of the Black Belt, there lived relatively isolated communities of white householders and their families who produced mainly for their own needs and had only occasional contact with the market economy. While their way of life distinguished these southern yeomen from the commercial farmers of the North, it also set them apart from the wealthier, less egalitarian planters of their own region; jealous of their personal independence and local autonomy, the southern yeomen resented any perceived intrusion on their political rights. White supremacy and the yeomen's acquiescence in slavery softened these class differences, but throughout the 1820s and 1830s the southern yeomen remained deeply suspicious of the planters' wealth and power, and the possibility that the planter elite might pursue local development policies to the detriment of the backcountry.

The rediscovery of the persistent southern yeomen—in contrast to the declining northern yeomen—has reinforced the argument for growing social divergence between North and South before 1850. But in a different sense the southern yeomen's dilemmas also point out certain commonalities in the history of commercialization throughout the country, which in turn help us understand the market revolution as a national process.

At one level, commercialization—as overseen by the nation's merchant capitalists, manufacturers, commercial farmers, and planters—created a hybrid political economy by introducing capitalist forms of labor and market agriculture in the North, and by fostering a different slave-based order in the South. Viewed more closely, the market revolution can also be seen to have produced new and potentially troublesome social conflicts within each major section of the country. Entrepreneurs and wage earners, middlemen and petty producers, masters and slaves, planters and yeomen all found themselves placed in unfamiliar positions, arrayed against each other in fresh struggles for power and legitimacy. In the long run the divergences between free labor and slavery would dominate other differences. Before then, however, new social relations and conflicts *within* the various sections generated social tensions that came to the fore in politics.

Understood in this way, the main lines of Jacksonian social and political history begin to look very different than they did to the consensus historians earlier. But in order to come to terms with these matters, historians have had to find out how Americans of different classes, races, and regions experienced the enormous structural changes that confronted them, and how they acted upon those new understandings. Few historians today would argue that economic interest alone determined people's views of the world. Jacksonian historians have found that Americans understood the market revolution as a cultural and political challenge, not simply an economic transformation. These findings have led to a thorough revision of key aspects of American intellectual history after 1815, especially on the contours of political ideology and social consciousness.

IDEOLOGY AND SOCIAL CONSCIOUSNESS

Much of the most important recent work on ideology and social consciousness after 1815 has focused on Americans whom previous generations thought of as "inarticulate"—including women, slaves, and workingmen. Combined with the history of the market revolution, efforts to study ideas "from the bottom up" have revealed far deeper and more complex divisions between various groups of Americans than were once supposed to have existed. Yet the most profound changes in our understanding of popular ideas have come from a larger reorientation in the ways historians approach early American social and political thought—above all, republican political ideas and the social meanings of evangelical Protestantism.

Studies of early nineteenth-century republicanism owe a great deal to some outstanding work, begun in the 1960s, on eighteenth-century politics and the origins and consequences of the American Revolution.

After surveying American political discourse at the nation's formation, such scholars as Bernard Bailyn, Richard Bushman, J. G. A. Pocock, and Gordon Wood found it difficult to sustain the widespread assumption that America's revolutionary ideology was essentially a pragmatic, legalistic variant of liberal capitalist ideas, derived mainly from John Locke. When late eighteenth-century Americans spoke of politics, they referred to a broad set of principles that they subsumed under the heading of republicanism.

Formulated in a world of monarchs and aristocrats, American republicanism was a radical, nearly utopian vision. Five interlocking concepts formed its key elements: first, that the ultimate goal of any political society should be the protection of the common good, or *commonwealth;* second, that in order to maintain this commonwealth, citizens had to exercise *virtue,* the ability to subordinate private ends to the public good when the two conflicted; third, that to be virtuous, citizens had to be *independent* of the political will of other men; fourth, that to guard against the rise of tyranny, citizens had to exercise their *citizenship* and be active in political life; fifth, that all citizens were entitled to *equality* under a representative, democratic system of laws. Some Americans emphasized certain of these concepts more than others; different groups interpreted them to mean different things; still, current historians argue that Americans drew primarily on these ideals in denouncing Old World inequality and in defining themselves as a nation.

The rediscovery of republicanism has sparked several debates with enormous implications for U.S. history after 1815. Joyce Appleby, for one, has warned against ignoring the prominence of liberal ideas about natural rights in early American political thought—ideas that Appleby thinks opened the way for a new capitalist order. Others have stressed the importance of plebeian democratic notions of the republic as spread among urban artisans and backwoods farmers—notions at odds in several respects with both traditional republican thought and with emerging capitalist liberalism. Still others have argued that republican ideas did not long survive the American Revolution as the mainspring of U.S. political thought. Lately, however, it has seemed that the demise of republican politics has been greatly exaggerated. Historians studying the nineteenth century have found that at least through the 1850s, republican political language proliferated throughout the United States. Rather than giving way to a kind of undifferentiated market liberalism, republicanism, it now seems, became a reference point of struggle as emergent classes identified their own interests with the survival and well-being of the republic itself.

Recent labor historians, for example, have found that many of the protest movements of the early nineteenth century proclaimed a distinct working-class republicanism, which combined republican ideals and the labor theory of value to touch the deepest emotions of the rank and file. At the heart of the matter was the question of whether the market revolution and its new forms of wage labor advanced or undermined republican ideals. To northern businessmen, commercialization was the handmaiden of republican progress: by increasing national wealth, they believed, entrepreneurs would widen opportunities for all honest and diligent workingmen to achieve virtuous independence. But to a growing number of workers, the market revolution seemed to vitiate republican ideals—by creating new forms of potentially awesome, undemocratic private power such as banks and corporations, by disrupting the supposedly mutualist regime of the artisan workshop, and by threatening workers with permanent dependence on wages and the capitalist labor market. At stake, organized workers argued, were not simply their own material interests (although these were important) but the fate of the republic in a land they thought had been overrun by purse-proud, nonproducing aristocrats and their political allies.

Similar themes appeared in very different settings as Americans interpreted their new, often bewildering circumstances in terms of the republican political legacy. Yeomen and would-be yeomen in the Northeast and the West attacked land speculators and bankers as an elite money power out to deprive farmers of their hard-won independence. Small producers in the South eyed both planters and merchants in southern cities as wealthy incipient aristocrats and tried to expand the political power of ordinary white men. By the 1830s this crisis of republican values, born of the market revolution, had produced popular movements for labor's rights, land reform, debtor relief, expansion of the suffrage, hard money, and numerous other causes. In response, northern businessmen, western speculators, and southern planters attempted in various ways to link their own favored position with the vindication of democratic republicanism.

Alongside these political divisions a deep spiritual and religious crisis also developed, loosely referred to as the Second Great Awakening. The theological implications of the evangelical revivals of the early nineteenth century and the decline of Calvinist orthodoxy was not lost on earlier generations of researchers; the religious ecstasy unleashed by the evangelicals' camp meetings have long fascinated social historians. But except in the work of a few pioneering scholars such as Whitney Cross, the larger social meanings of the revival were usually described—vaguely—as manifestations of an alleged Jacksonian democratic spirit. Historians today are much more exact; the rise of evangelicalism in its many forms seems to have been critical to the social and ideological transformations that accompanied the market revolution.

Nowhere did the revivals have a more profound impact than in those commercializing rural areas of the North and West familiarly known as the Burned-Over District. Building on the work of Cross, Paul Johnson and Mary Ryan have carefully reconstructed the sociology of northern evangelicalism. Focusing on Charles Finney's revival in Rochester, New York, Johnson found that it was initially a movement of and for business-men, commercial farmers, and their families. In the new measures and liberalized doctrines of conversion of the Finneyites' free churches, John-son argues, these people discovered both religious explanations for the breakdown of old interpersonal community relations and a new vision of man and God, consonant with the middle-class virtues of regular indus-try, sobriety, and self-reliance. Ryan, in a study of Utica, New York, pays closer attention to the gender dimension of the revivals and emphasizes that the majority of evangelical converts through the 1830s were the wives and daughters of businessmen; while serving as "the cradle of the middle class," Ryan concludes, the revivals had the more immediate consequence of helping to forge a religious view of sexual gentility and female spiri-tual worth in line with emerging forms of domesticity and middle-class respectability. The evangelical awakening seems to have provided a means whereby the new northern middle class forged the moral imperatives that defined them as a class. And once they did that, the evangelized converts (especially women) attempted with uneven success to bring the rest of society into the fold by means of urban missions, Bible societies, and a host of other religiously inspired moral reform efforts.

The revivals came even earlier to the South than to the North and had, if anything, a more pervasive influence—but their social signifi-cance was rather different. Slaveholders, particularly those born outside the established eastern upper crust, found in the teachings of various Bap-tist, Methodist, and New School Presbyterians a promise of spiritual rebirth and a potential instrument for "civilizing" (and thus further subordinating) their slaves. However, as such scholars as Donald Mathews have explained, the social meaning of southern evangelicalism steadily diverged from that of the northern churches—and, in an important respect, from the slave-holders' own original intentions. Northern evangelicals, with their bedrock insistence on human equality before God, the sinfulness of human coer-cion, and individual responsibility, generated passions that easily took on antislavery connotations. Southern planters could not accept such views and did not permit them in their churches. Instead, southern evangelical-ism came to accept the inferiority of blacks and to emphasize the slave-holders' supposed civilizing mission as a form of Christian stewardship. The slaves, however, although drawn to evangelical Christianity, did not take from it the submissive message the slaveholders thought they would. On the contrary, they blended the biblical motifs of exodus and redemp-tion with surviving West African religious customs and made of them a foundation of their own sense of dignity and community.

Taken together, the continued fragmentation of American republicanism and the ferment of the revivals reveal an intricate series of social and ideological redefinitions. Armed with these views, Americans struggled over the basic issues raised by commercialization, interpreting their conflicts as battles for the very soul of the nation. These struggles shaped the political tumults and innovations associated with the age of Jackson.

POLITICS

It is in the area of politics that the recent historiography of the Jacksonian era may seem the most confused. In the 1960s, revisionist political historians were heralding a revolution in methodology and interpretation. Using formidable statistical hardware and the sociological tools of multivariate analysis, the "new" political historians proclaimed as their major finding that, contrary to then prevailing interpretations, economics and class had played only limited roles in shaping political alignments. Ethnicity, culture, and religion, it turned out, were the keys to understanding Jacksonian politics.

These revisionist accounts swept away the mechanistic, often one-dimensional instrumentalism that had marred earlier social interpretations of Jacksonian politics. Yet in the years since this academic revolution began, historians (including some of the "new" political historians) have had second thoughts. Their conclusions did not work for every area of the country; even where they appeared to be valid, the divorce of class factors from culture and ethnicity began to seem artificial. A few efforts at correcting such problems have tried to combine the worthy findings of the "new" political history with those of recent social historians, and out of this work have come more convincing appraisals of the overlapping effects of class, culture, and political ideology. Even more important, these studies have broadened the scope of political history to cover not simply electoral contests and voting returns but the entire way in which power was structured and restructured after 1815.

An important early development in this new social history of politics was a full reevaluation of the origins of professional parties, notably in Richard Hofstadter's 1969 book on changing concepts of party from the framing of the Constitution through the 1820s. Inspired partly by the rediscovery of eighteenth-century republican political discourse, Hofstadter demonstrated how deeply the Founding Fathers abhorred the idea of permanent party divisions, regarding them as factionalized solvents of the commonwealth. Even Thomas Jefferson, head of the first national opposition party in American history, had no intention of making party divisions permanent. Jefferson's celebrated remarks at his first inaugural—"We are all Federalists, we are all Republicans"—meant that in his view only one party, his own, was needed. This anti-party animus lasted down to the 1820s, only to be challenged by a new generation of political upstarts, among them future Jacksonian strategists such as Martin Van Buren. Drawn largely from outside the traditional elite gentry families, this new breed of politicians believed that without regularly organized parties the nation would fall into either unceasing civil strife or oligarchy. Political conflict, they insisted, was inevitable in a nation so diverse as the United States; to deny the expression of that conflict through regular, legitimate channels was both foolhardy and dangerous. Only a forthrightly competitive system of organized parties, each responsible to a broad white male electorate and a party rank and file, and each led by professional politicians, could ensure political stability and legislate the popular will.

The emergence of these new kinds of politicians helped to ventilate the political system, at both local and national levels, by encouraging the expansion of the suffrage and important reforms in representation in states still attached to eighteenth-century property requirements. By 1830 the vast majority of the states had either adopted or moved decisively toward universal adult white male suffrage. This process of democratization—discriminating and oppressive as it was to women and free blacks—did not, however, proceed simply from the idealistic or benevolent efforts of new and emerging political elites. Considerable pressure at the grassroots—particularly from the plebeian backcountry—often instigated democratic reform; once organized, this pressure from below often pushed the politician-reformers to proceed well beyond what they initially expected to achieve.

Shifts in national policy, meanwhile, further exacerbated popular discontent. With the demise of the Federalist party after the War of 1812, it appeared to many as if Jeffersonian principles of frugal government and strict construction of the Constitution had at last been vindicated. Yet partly as a result of the mobilization for the war, elements within the Jeffersonian coalition more friendly to government-supported economic development had begun to gain the upper hand. By the mid-1820s many of these men, joined by ex-Federalists, had started to coalesce in a loose-knit way as what would soon be called National Republicans—shorn of much of the belligerent, elitist animus of the old Federalist party but interested in using national institutions (including the Second Bank of the United States, chartered in 1816) to expand the market revolution. In the presidential election of 1824, John Quincy Adams, a leading figure in this group, emerged the winner—though only after the election was thrown into the House of Representatives, where it was beclouded with charges of backroom deals and corruption. Suddenly—or so it seemed to some observers—a revamped form of New England Federalism had captured the White House.

In the aftermath of Adams's election, most of the new party professionals gravitated toward the oppositional presidential aspirations of Andrew Jackson; as much as anything, Jackson's eventual election to the presidency in 1828 amounted to a triumph for the professional vision of party politics. It was to prove only the beginning of a tremendous political transformation. Although known to be unfriendly to various National Republican measures, Jackson ran for the White House on his popularity as a military hero rather than on any clearly defined issues. Even as he was sworn into office, it was not altogether clear where he and his newly formed party would stand on the various political controversies of the day. Nor was it clear how Jackson's adversaries would respond, except to announce their opposition to the professional party idea and their distrust (in some cases, detestation) of Andrew Jackson.

The events that shaped the new political alignments—what historians have dubbed the second of the nation's "party systems"—were directly connected to the social tensions of the market revolution. They came with extraordinary rapidity in the years immediately before and after Jackson's election. Labor conflict hit the Northeast on an unprecedented scale as workers and their radical friends organized the first national labor movement—initially with a string of locally based workingmen's parties, then in centralized urban unions and a national trades' union. Employers responded to union activities with their own organizations and with legal prosecutions aimed effectively at denying workers the right to strike. In 1831 the northern revival reached a crescendo with the Finneyite eruption in Rochester; throughout the decade, evangelized middle-class northerners joined churches and religious moral reform societies by the hundreds of thousands. Western small farmers and squatters pressed for reform of public land policy to widen and guarantee their access to the land. Nat Turner's slave rebellion in 1831 touched off a wave of legal repression in the South to prevent any further such insurrections and to uproot antislavery opinion. Southern yeomen joined popular movements demanding further democratization of the suffrage and wider eligibility for officeholding in some of the older slave states.

Against this background the Jacksonians assembled their party constituency and ideology. Jackson himself was a central figure in this process, if only as a popular symbol; current historians have hotly debated exactly what Jackson stood for. In a study heavily influenced by Freudian insights, Jackson's fiercest critic, Michael Paul Rogin, has portrayed the Old Hero as a deeply disturbed man whose need to supplant the generation of the revolutionary fathers bred a pathologically violent character, its violence directed in particular at Native Americans. In contrast, Jackson's most thorough biographer, Robert V. Remini, has presented him as a politician and statesman who in many respects deserves to be remembered as a man of the people. Yet despite their clashing interpretations, Rogin and Remini (and historians generally) agree that Jackson and his party drew upon the old republican language and reworked it into a powerful political appeal.

Essentially, Jacksonianism developed as an expression of the fears and aspirations of those petty producers and workers threatened by commercialization, as well as of voters in outlying areas not yet integrated into the market revolution. This did not mean, historians are now quick to add, that the Democracy was simply a farmer-labor party, organized as a clear-cut opposition to merchant speculators and wealthy planters. Wealthy men (such as Jackson himself) commanded key party posts throughout the country; among them were men who helped to further the market revolution. Significant numbers of petty producers and wage earners, meanwhile, voted for the Democracy's opponents. Like all successful national parties in U.S. history, both the Democrats and the Whigs were coalitions of diverse social groups. For the most part, though, the Democracy tapped into the attitudes—and won the votes—of northern petty artisans and workers, marginal and middling farmers in the Northeast and Northwest, and southern yeomen. Democrats assumed that there was an inherent conflict between "producers" and "nonproducers," in which entrenched "nonproducers" would seek to use the power of the state to their own advantage. The Democrats' professed aim was not, therefore, to end all economic improvement and expansion but rather to keep the hands of established wealth and privilege off the levers of state power, thereby preventing the creation of a new and permanent monied aristocracy.

Jackson's war on the Second Bank of the United States was a turning-point in the building of his party's constituency and identity; his veto message brilliantly rearticulated the old republican discourse into a ringing defense of small producers against the alleged schemes of merchant capitalist financiers and foreign investors to subvert the Constitution and equal rights. Jackson's veto of federally sponsored internal improvements, along with Democratic congressional efforts for comprehensive land reform, likewise arrayed the "bone and sinew" against those private interests that would bend government to enhance their private power.

Jackson's enemies had difficulty organizing a coherent national opposition to this democratic appeal. Several studies have stressed that the anti-Jacksonians inherited the once prevalent distrust of political parties, which naturally hampered their responses to the Democrats. More important, as John Ashworth has pointed out, anti-Jacksonians tended to distrust electoral democracy altogether as a potential form of demagogic tyranny. Only in the late 1830s did the anti-Jacksonians finally learn to adapt to the realities of mass democratic politics and pull together as a national political force—the Whig party. Once organized, the Whigs completed a major shift in American political conservatism.

Central to Whig thinking was the desire for an orderly and regulated consolidation of the market revolution. Updating ideas elaborated by the Hamiltonian Federalists and the National Republicans, Whig leaders expected that with the prudent aid of an active, paternalist government (through banking policy, tariffs, and corporate charters), private capital would flourish, making the American economy truly independent of the Old World. Not surprisingly, this stance won considerable approval from northern businessmen, western capitalist farmers, and the larger southern planters. But what turned the Whigs from a poorly organized band into a powerful national party was the larger social and moral vision they attached to their prodevelopment economics and promulgated in their new party organization.

Rejecting the Democrats' claims of an inherent conflict between producers and nonproducers, the Whigs asserted that a basic harmony of interests united all Americans in a kind of mutualist whole. The enlargement of national wealth, they contended, would eventually bring greater opportunity for all. Since, the United States, unlike Britain and Europe, was a classless society, they insisted, all those who exhibited industry, thrift, and self-reliance could expect to earn their personal independence. Poverty and inequality, according to the Whigs, stemmed from individual moral failings, not from any flaws in existing political or economic structures. Reflecting both the ethical injunctions of the Second Great Awakening and the discourse of democratic republicanism, the Whigs' argument effectively presented the political and social consequences of the market revolution as the fulfillment of America's republican destiny. It won them considerable popular support from aspiring northern and western small producers, more fortunate wage earners, and some smaller southern planters and entrepreneurs.

By 1840 the clash between Democrats and Whigs had developed into a new party system of two fairly evenly matched national organizations. The politics of economic development remained at the center of their electoral and legislative battles—yet as recent work has emphasized, these battles expressed intense cultural conflicts as well. In the Northeast, for example, the Whigs' combination of economic and moral appeals struck home with Protestant workers and small producers, particularly those caught up in the revivals. Catholic immigrants, especially Irish Catholics at the bottom of the new labor market, were repelled by the Whigs' cultural politics and stuck with the Jacksonians. In the Northwest and the South the clash between the Democracy's emphasis on equal rights and the Whigs' emphasis on respectability set voters enmeshed in the semiautonomous world of the yeomen's communities against those country and city voters more thoroughly integrated into the commercial world. Particularly in the North, these strains surfaced in battles over all sorts of "cultural" issues without any apparent economic logic—temperance, sabbatarianism, nativism, common schooling—with the Whigs taking up the banner of moral reform. Throughout, however, the lines of class, ethnicity, religion, and subregion tended to converge; cultural identities in politics —the Whigs' entrepreneurial moralism versus the Democrats' stress on personal autonomy and equal rights—were inseparable from the ways in which the market revolution was threatening old ways of life, creating new ones, and setting large groups of Americans at odds.

As it happened, these battles were to be overshadowed by the even deeper struggles that emerged in the 1840s and eventually destroyed the second party system. The essential issue was the expansion of slavery; since 1970, historians have greatly enhanced our understanding of how slavery and antislavery came to dominate the political agenda. Numerous studies have established that both the Democrats and the Whigs understood the need to keep issues associated with slavery out of national affairs in order to ensure national party stability. The Constitutional Convention of 1787 and the Missouri Crisis of 1819–21 had shown that this was not always easy to do; the social consequences of the market revolution made the task even harder. The rise of the cotton South and the consolidation of planter power made that region increasingly touchy about any perceived threats to the peculiar institution, especially as the perceived common interest of planter and yeoman in the perpetuation of slavery became the most powerful bond for white southerners across the lines of class and party. In the North, meanwhile, the moral reform efforts that stemmed from the Second Great Awakening and the formation of the new middle class dramatically changed the thrust of antislavery opinion. Out of the maelstrom of reform emerged a new form of antislavery dedicated to "immediate" abolition— a far more radical prospect than anything proposed by the preceding antislavery organizations. Benefiting from the organizational structure of what one historian has called the benevolent empire of reform, and borrowing from propaganda techniques of the revivalist churches, the immediatist abolitionists began to win hundreds of thousands of converts in the most rapidly expanding areas of northern development.

The potential divisiveness of these events did not become fully apparent until after 1840. Before that, party leaders had successfully turned away attempts by both sides to inject slavery into national affairs, using compromise where possible, the threat of force when necessary (as in Jackson's handling of the Nullification Crisis of 1832–33), and parliamentary repression (as in the adoption of the gag rule in 1838).

Two political developments helped alter the situation. First, one wing of the abolitionist movement rejected the position of William Lloyd Garrison and others who held that reformers should remain outside politics. Members of this wing entered party politics for themselves and began to adapt their antislavery views to broader public opinion. Second, internal disputes within the Democracy set the northern and southern wings of the party at odds, amid claims that southern interests (led by the sectional firebrand John C. Calhoun) intended to take over. Both developments made it difficult for party leaders to return to the kinds of issues that had given rise to the second party system. In the mid-1840s the entire system was shaken when debates over Texas annexation and the Mexican War reopened the kinds of territorial issues that had always been rife with sectional antagonism. By 1848 sectional passions dogged the nation's politics on an alarming scale—passions emblematized when the antislavery Free Soil Party ran on its national ticket two leading figures of the political establishment: the Democratic former president, Martin Van Buren, and the Massachusetts Whig (and son of a former president, John Quincy Adams) Charles Francis Adams.

It would, of course, take another six years before the second party system finally fell apart, and six more after that before the nation was severed. The political generation of Jackson was able to reconstruct intersectional party alliances, at least in Congress; antislavery northerners and southern sectionalists still had a long way to go in building sectional majorities. Yet by 1848 the political impetus behind the Jacksonian party system was quickly exhausting itself. The social and ideological transformations that had given birth to the Jacksonian Democracy and the Whigs continued —but their significance changed as the deeper sectional implications of economic development became paramount.

Here lay the ultimate paradox of the age. The market revolution, having disrupted old social relations and created new ideological and spiritual crises, encouraged the emergence of a new form of mass democratic party politics. Once in place, the second party system revolved around certain intrasectional issues of class and culture linked to the impact of commercialization. Yet the market revolution also widened the social differences between the free-labor North and the slave South. Once those differences entered national politics—agitated by sectional politicians skilled in the techniques of mass democracy—they threatened the very existence of the second party system. The nation's politicians could not forever contain struggles over the meaning of such grand concepts as equality, independence, and individual autonomy in ways that circumvented the fundamental problems raised by the expansion of slavery. In the 1850s and 1860s, Americans would reap the whirlwind.

BIBLIOGRAPHY

This list covers only some of the noteworthy books published since the mid-1970s, plus a few key works from the 1950s and 1960s. Books that might prove useful in the classroom are marked with an asterisk.

Appleby, Joyce O. *Capitalism and a New Social Order: The Republican Version of the 1790s.* New York: New York University Press, 1984.

Ashworth, John. *Agrarians and Aristocrats: Party Ideology in the United States, 1837–1846.* Wolfeboro, N.H.: Longwood, 1983.

Bailyn, Bernard. *The Ideological Origins of the American Revolution.* Cambridge, Mass.: Harvard University Press, 1967.

Berlin, Ira. *Slaves without Masters: The Free Negro in the Antebellum South.* New York: Pantheon Books, 1974.

*Blassingame, John W. *The Slave Community: Plantation Life in the Antebellum South.* Rev. ed. New York: Oxford University Press, 1979.

Boyer, Paul. *Urban Masses and Moral Order in America, 1820–1920.* Cambridge, Mass.: Harvard University Press, 1978.

Bridges, Amy. *A City in the Republic: New York and the Origins of Machine Politics.* New York: Cambridge University Press, 1984.

Bushman, Richard L. *King and People in Provincial Massachusetts.* Chapel Hill: University of North Carolina Press, 1985.

Cole, Donald B. *Martin Van Buren and the American Political System.* Princeton, N.J.: Princeton University Press, 1984.

Cooper, William J. *The South and the Politics of Slavery, 1828–1856.* Baton Rouge: Louisiana State University Press, 1978.

*Cott, Nancy F. *The Bonds of Womanhood: "Woman's Sphere" in New England, 1780–1835.* New Haven, Conn.: Yale University Press, 1977.

Cross, Whitney. *The Burned-Over District: The Social and Intellectual History of Enthusiastic Religion in Western New York.* Ithaca, N.Y.: Cornell University Press, 1950.

Dawley, Alan. *Class and Community: The Industrial Revolution in Lynn.* Cambridge, Mass.: Harvard University Press, 1976.

Douglas, Ann. *The Feminization of American Culture.* New York: Knopf, 1977.

Doyle, Don H. *The Social Order of a Frontier Community: Jacksonville, Illinois, 1825–70.* Urbana: University of Illinois Press, 1978.

Dublin, Thomas. *Women at Work: The Transformation of Work and Community in Lowell, Massachusetts, 1826–1860.* New York: Columbia University Press, 1979.

Faler, Paul G. *Mechanics and Manufacturers in the Early Industrial Revolution: Lynn, Massachusetts, 1780–1860.* Albany: State University of New York Press, 1981.

Foner, Eric. *Politics and Ideology in the Age of the Civil War.* New York: Oxford University Press, 1980.

Formisano, Ronald P. *The Transformation of Political Culture: Massachusetts Parties, 1790s–1840s.* New York: Oxford University Press, 1983.

Foster, Lawrence. *Religion and Sexuality: Three American Communal Experiments in the Nineteenth Century.* New York: Oxford University Press, 1981.

Genovese, Eugene D. *Roll, Jordan, Roll: The World the Slaves Made.* New York: Pantheon Books, 1974.

Gutman, Herbert G. *The Black Family in Slavery and Freedom, 1750–1925.* New York: Pantheon Books, 1976.

———. *Work, Culture, and Society in Industrializing America: Essays in American Working-Class History.* New York: Knopf, 1976.

Hahn, Steven. *The Roots of Southern Populism: Yeoman Farmers and the Transformation of the Georgia Upcountry, 1850–1890.* New York: Oxford University Press, 1983.

Hofstadter, Richard. *The Idea of a Party System: The Rise of Legitimate Opposition in the United States, 1780–1840.* Berkeley: University of California Press, 1969.

Horwitz, Morton J. *The Transformation of American Law, 1780–1860.* Cambridge, Mass.: Harvard University Press, 1977.

Howe, Daniel Walker. *The Political Culture of the American Whigs.* Chicago: University of Chicago Press, 1979.

Jensen, Joan. *Loosening the Bonds: Mid-Atlantic Farm Women, 1750–1850.* New Haven, Conn.: Yale University Press, 1986.

*Johnson, Paul E. *A Shopkeeper's Millennium: Society and Revival in Rochester, New York, 1815–1837.* New York: Hill & Wang, 1978.

Kelley, Robert L. *The Cultural Pattern in American Politics: The First Century.* New York: Knopf, 1979.

Laurie, Bruce G. *Working People of Philadelphia, 1800–1850.* Philadelphia: Temple University Press, 1980.

*Levine, Lawrence W. *Black Culture and Black Consciousness: Afro-American Folk Thought from Slavery to Freedom.* New York: Oxford University Press, 1977.

Lindstrom, Diane. *Economic Development in the Philadelphia Region, 1810–1850.* New York: Columbia University Press, 1978.

Mathews, Donald G. *Religion in the Old South.* Chicago: University of Chicago Press, 1977.

Oakes, James. *The Ruling Race: A History of American Slaveholders.* New York: Knopf, 1982.

Pessen, Edward. *Riches, Class, and Power before the Civil War.* Lexington, Mass.: Heath, 1973.

Peterson, Merrill D. *The Great Triumvirate: Webster, Clay, and Calhoun.* New York: Oxford University Press, 1987.

Raboteau, Albert J. *Slave Religion: The Invisible Institution in the Antebellum South.* New York: Oxford University Press, 1978.

Remini, Robert V. *Andrew Jackson and the Course of American Democracy, 1833–1845,* vol. 3. New York: Harper & Row, 1984.

Rogin, Michael. *Fathers and Children: Andrew Jackson and the Subjugation of the American Indian.* New York: Knopf, 1975.

Rorabaugh, W. J. *The Alcoholic Republic: An American Tradition.* New York: Oxford University Press, 1979.

Ross, Steven J. *Workers on the Edge: Work, Leisure, and Politics in Industrializing Cincinnati, 1788–1890.* New York: Columbia University Press, 1985.

Ryan, Mary P. *Cradle of the Middle Class: The Family in Oneida County, New York, 1790–1865.* New York: Cambridge University Press, 1983.

Satz, Ronald N. *American Indian Policy in the Jacksonian Era*. Lincoln: University of Nebraska Press, 1975.

Smith-Rosenberg, Carroll. *Disorderly Conduct: Visions of Gender in Victorian America*. New York: Knopf, 1985.

Stansell, Christine. *City of Women: Sex and Class in New York, 1789–1860*. New York: Knopf, 1986.

*Stewart, James B. *Holy Warriors: The Abolitionists and American Slavery*. New York: Hill & Wang, 1976.

Taylor, George Rogers. *The Transportation Revolution, 1815–1860*. White Plains, N.Y.: M. E. Sharpe, 1951.

Thornton, J. Mills, III. *Politics and Power in a Slave Society: Alabama, 1800–1860*. Baton Rouge: Louisiana State University Press, 1978.

Wallace, Anthony F. C. *Rockdale: The Growth of an American Village in the Early Industrial Revolution*. New York: Knopf, 1978.

*Walters, Ronald G. *American Reformers, 1815–1860*. New York: Hill & Wang, 1978.

Watson, Harry L. *Jacksonian Politics and Community Conflict: The Emergence of the Second American Party System in Cumberland County, North Carolina*. Baton Rouge: Louisiana State University Press, 1981.

Wiebe, Robert H. *The Opening of American Society: From the Adoption of the Constitution to the Eve of Disunion*. New York: Knopf, 1984.

Wilentz, Sean. *Chants Democratic: New York City & the Rise of the American Working Class, 1788–1850*. New York: Oxford University Press, 1984.